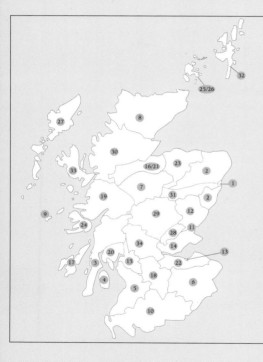

1. Aberdeen
2. Aberdeenshire
3. Argyll
4. The Isle of Arran
5. Arran & Ayrshire
6. The Borders
7. The Cairngorms
8. Caithness & Sutherland
9. Coll & Tiree
10. Dumfries & Galloway
11. Dundee
12. Dundee & Angus
13. Edinburgh
14. Fife, Kinross & Clackmannan
15. Glasgow
16. Inverness
17. Islay, Jura, Colonsay & Oronsay

18. Lanarkshire
19. Lochaber
20. Loch Lomond, Cowal & Bute
21. Loch Ness
22. The Lothians
23. Moray-Speyside
24. Mull & Iona
25. Orkney
26. Orkney in Wartime
27. The Outer Hebrides
28. The City of Perth
29. Highland Perthshire
30. Ross & Cromarty
31. Royal Deeside
32. Shetland
33. The Isle of Skye
34. Stirling & The Trossachs

The remaining six books, *Caledonia*, *Distinguished Distilleries*, *Sacred Scotland*, *Scotland's Mountains*, *Scotland's Wildlife* and *The West Highland Way* feature locations in various parts of the country, so are not included in the map list above.

*PICTURING SCOTLAND*

# ORKNEY IN WARTIME

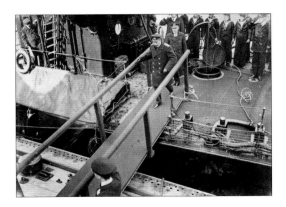

COLIN NUTT
Author and photographer

**2** The view south-east from Wideford Hill on Orkney's Mainland, with Scapa Flow on the right. Orkney's south-eastern islands stretch into the distance with one of the Churchill Barriers just visible.

# ORKNEY IN WARTIME

# Introduction

Orkney has played a pivotal role in the defence of the British Isles in major conflicts over many years. The huge haven of Scapa Flow has provided safe anchorage for ships for centuries and the Royal Navy based scores of vessels there in both World Wars. At times during the First World War the number of naval personnel in Orkney reached 100,000. To put that figure in perspective, the present-day population of Orkney is approximately 21,600.

Orkney is geologically spectacular, archaeologically unsurpassed (in Scotland) and historically fascinating. The pattern of islands that makes up Orkney begins about six miles north of Caithness on the Scottish mainland, separated from it by the frequently turbulent Pentland Firth. From southern tip to northernmost point is a straight-line distance of approximately 50 miles, but requires a journey by road and ferry of several hours.

Scapa Flow is the area of sea largely surrounded by Orkney's southern islands. It amounts to approximately 120 square miles and is protected by the islands of South Ronaldsay, Flotta and Walls to the south, Hoy to the west and Orkney's Mainland to the north. It is one of the largest natural harbours in the world and has been used by ships seeking shelter over many centuries. The Vikings knew the Flow well and called it Skalpafloi. In 1263, with Scotland challenging Norwegian rule of the Hebrides, King Håkon brought his great Viking Fleet of some 120 large ships east across the North Sea in a bid to maintain Norwegian hegemony (rule by force). They anchored off St Margaret's Hope in Scapa Flow, before sailing south via Cape Wrath to Largs on the River Clyde estuary. The ensuing battle with the Scots under King Alexander III was not conclusive but thereafter Norwegian influence began to wane. The ailing Håkon and his fleet limped back to Orkney, where the king died in the Bishop's Palace in Kirkwall.

During the Napoleonic Wars, Scapa Flow was an important convoy assembly point for British vessels trading with the Baltic countries. Hackness Battery and Martello Tower were built in 1813–14, at the height of the Napoleonic Wars. America had declared war on Britain in 1812 in pursuit of independence and both French and American warships were wreaking havoc on British and Scandinavian merchant shipping going 'north about' through the Pentland Firth or round Orkney. Longhope Sound provided a safe anchorage. The battery at Hackness was built first, followed by two Martello towers – Hackness (just 200m from the battery) and Crockness on the north side of the Sound.

The Bishop's Palace in Kirkwall where King Håkon died after the Battle of Largs.

As the war clouds gathered in the early 20th Century and Britain acknowledged the threat of the German High Seas Fleet, a northern base was sought for the British Grand Fleet. After a series of manoeuvres around Orkney and, largely because of the enthusiasm of Lord Fisher and Admiral Jellicoe, the natural anchorage of Scapa Flow was chosen in 1912 to be this base.

This book sets out to summarise the role that Orkney in general, and Scapa Flow in particular, played in providing a home for the Royal Navy in both World Wars. A particular emphasis is on the week from 31st May to 6th June 1916 during the First World War, a fateful period in which the Battle of Jutland was fought and HMS *Hampshire* was sunk while attempting to take Lord Kitchener on a diplomatic mission to meet the Tsar in Russia. After examining further WW1 incidents, the book moves forward to the Second World War, in which Orkney played a similar role in supporting the Royal Navy.

**6**  Crockness Martello Tower on the north side of Longhope Sound, built during the Napoleonic Wars.

Many of the coastal fortifications that remain so prominent today date from this conflict. Most notable among these are the Churchill Barriers, hastily constructed soon after the outbreak of war to keep German submarines out of Scapa Flow after one of them was responsible for sinking HMS *Royal Oak* in 1939. Once built, the four barriers effectively created land bridges that connected the islands of Lamb Holm, Glimps Holm, Burray and South Ronaldsay, greatly improving communications in this part of Orkney. Today's road crosses the barriers (see pp.71 & 74).

To illustrate these events and their setting, the book uses a mix of black and white archive images and present-day colour photographs intended to show the scenic side of Orkney in areas where these historic events took place. It is hoped that this approach to illustration and the accompanying text will make some small contribution to commemorating the centenaries of the WW1 events mentioned above, while showcasing the splendour of the Orkney Islands themselves.

HMS *Hampshire's* quarter deck and crew.

8    A remarkable picture of the Home Fleet in Scapa Flow, given that it was taken at midnight over a century ago. Granted, it was taken on 20th June, a time of year in Orkney when it does not get

completely dark. It is quite possibly a unique image, apart from any others the photographer may have taken on the same occasion.

## Scapa Flow – home of the Grand Fleet

The Grand Fleet sailed into Scapa Flow in July 1914, just weeks before Britain declared war on Germany and what would become the First World War began. HMS *Iron Duke* was the flagship, under the command of Admiral Sir George Callaghan. Although he was due to retire in December, the Admiralty planned to replace him immediately. Admiral Sir John Jellicoe travelled from London by overnight train, arriving in Wick on the morning of 1st August. At this point, even he did not know what was intended, believing he was going to be Callaghan's second-in-command.

However, on the 4th August (the day Britain declared war on Germany), Jellicoe opened the sealed orders he had been handed on leaving London and found what he had in fact begun to suspect: he was the new Commander-in-Chief of the Grand Fleet. The fleet comprised 20 dreadnoughts, four battle-cruisers, 42 destroyers and eight older ships.

Scapa Flow was not well defended against incursions from enemy vessels at the start of the war. Indeed, Jellicoe wondered why the German navy did not mount an attack in those early days. In the relatively close confines of the Flow, the 74 ships stationed there would be sitting ducks, especially if a U-boat got amongst them. To guard against this risk, Jellicoe kept the ships at sea as much as possible in the early days of the conflict.

Although being at sea, and therefore dispersed over a much wider area, reduced the danger of having many ships attacked at once, they were then prone to other risks. For the most part this meant mines, 43,000 of which were laid by the Germans over the course of the war. The navy had very few minesweepers at the start of the war and consequently had to commandeer local fishing boats to undertake this dangerous work. While the technique of dealing with mines was being learnt, one trawler was sunk for every two mines cleared. Many Orcadian fishermen, working alongside naval officers, served with distinction in this role over the course of the conflict.

Admiral Sir John Jellicoe, Commander-in-Chief of the Grand Fleet. **11**

12 The view north-east from Cuilags hill on the island of Hoy. Stromness is on the left,
Hoy Sound is in the foreground, leading to Scapa Flow away to the right.

Broadly speaking, this is the reverse view, looking across the Bring Deeps 13
(between Scapa Flow and Hoy Sound) towards Cuilags.

## The Battle of Jutland

The British Grand Fleet was larger than the German High Seas Fleet, but, ship by ship, there was little to choose between the relative merits of the two. They had different strengths and weaknesses. While much could be gained for the winning side if a clear-cut victory was the outcome, defeat would be more serious for the British than the Germans: Britain's island status made it much more dependent on imported food, raw materials and other supplies in general. Britain also needed a large navy to protect her colonies and to protect supplies being sent to the army fighting in France.

Above all, a strong navy was necessary to protect Britain itself from invasion and to protect merchant shipping. Engaging in a pitched battle with the Germans could be viewed as a vanity project rather than an absolute need. If the Royal Navy lost too many ships in such an exchange, the German navy would be able to cut off Britain's vital supplies. Conversely, destruction of the German High Seas Fleet would not inflict great harm on Germany's war effort. Winston Churchill, First Sea Lord at the time, summed it up succinctly by saying that 'Admiral Jellicoe is the only commander on either side who is capable of losing the war in a single afternoon'. Whether Churchill was merely expressing a simple truth as he saw it, or expressing a veiled reservation about Jellicoe's abilities is a matter of conjecture.

**14**  Opposite: HMS *Iron Duke* (left) and three minesweepers in Scapa Flow. She was flagship of the Grand Fleet from August 1914 to January 1917. She survived the Battle of Jutland unscathed but

was later damaged in an air raid while in the Flow and, although she looks as though she is afloat, is actually resting on the sea-bed in this picture.

Both Jellicoe and his opposite number, Vice-Admiral Reinhard Scheer, wanted to avoid a pitched battle unless assured of victory. As, of course, no such assurance could be given, both men were cagey about engaging their fleets. So it was that the war was fought with little in the way of major naval engagements until May 1916. On 30th May, the German High Seas Fleet massed to start operations against British merchant shipping in the Skagerrak between Norway and Denmark, hoping to tempt some of the British forces into a dangerous position. Although it was the only major naval battle of World War I, it became the largest sea battle in naval warfare history in terms of the numbers of battleships and battle-cruisers engaged, bringing together the two most powerful naval forces in existence at that time.

Word of the German manoeuvre came through from Naval Intelligence in the early evening of 30th May. In response, the British Grand Fleet steamed eastwards across the North Sea in two groups – the battle-cruiser fleet commanded by Admiral Sir David Beatty from its base at Rosyth and the main battle fleet under Admiral Sir John Jellicoe, from its base at Scapa Flow. The German High Seas Fleet moved northwards from Wilhelmshaven in a similar formation, with Admiral Franz Hipper's faster battle-cruisers steaming ahead of the main battle fleet under Vice-Admiral Reinhard Scheer. By early morning of 31st May 1916, the British and German fleets were on a collision course but, incredibly, neither knew that the other was at sea. Scheer was unaware that his signals were being intercepted, whilst Jellicoe and Beatty were mistakenly informed by the Admiralty at midday that Scheer was still in harbour at Wilhelmshaven. Consequently, when visual contact was made by the advance battle-cruisers of Beatty and Hipper at 14.40, this came as a surprise to both sides. The time-line of the battle continues as follows:

**Key:**

Beatty

Scheer

Hipper

**15.30:** Beatty sights Hipper's leading battle-cruisers. Hipper turns towards the south-east, hoping to lure Beatty in the direction of Scheer's main battle fleet which is 50 miles to the south and closing rapidly. At this point, Scheer and Hipper must have thought that their plan to detach Beatty from the main British fleet was working.

17

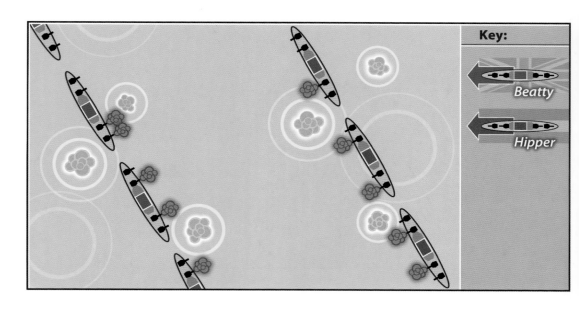

**Key:**

Beatty

Hipper

**18  15.48:** both sides open fire. Almost immediately, HMS *Indefatigable* is blown up and sunk with the loss of all but two of her crew.

HMS *Indefatigable*, first victim of the Battle of Jutland. As noted opposite, only two of her crew survived, but records vary as to the numbers on board, from 900 to 1,119.

**20** HMS *Queen Mary* receives a direct hit on her magazine. She explodes and sinks. From a crew of 2,000 only 20 survive. In little over half-an-hour, around 3,000 British sailors have been lost.

**Key:**

Beatty

Scheer

Hipper

**16.40:** Beatty sights the German High Seas Fleet in the distance and turns his battle-cruisers northwards to avoid the German trap. He sets his own by drawing Scheer and Hipper towards **21** Jellicoe and the British Grand Fleet which is rapidly approaching from the north-west.

**Key:**

Jellicoe

Scheer

Beatty

Hipper

**17.35:** whilst escaping to the north-west, Beatty continues to engage Hipper's cruisers, forcing them 22 further east. Unable to see the approaching British Grand Fleet, the whole German fleet is about to enter the trap Jellicoe and Beatty have prepared.

H.M.S. "MARLBOROUGH."

HMS *Marlborough* was an Iron Duke-class battleship launched in 1912. She fought at the Battle of **23** Jutland where she was hit by a German torpedo which killed two men and injured two more.

**18.05:** Jellicoe Jellicoe sights the battle-cruiser action from a distance of 15 miles. With little information from Beatty and not being sure exactly where Scheer was, Jellicoe has to decide how to deploy his fleet from cruising mode to battle formation.

**18.15:** Jellicoe decides to deploy his battleships to port (left) to form a single line behind the port column. This has been described as 'the Royal Navy's most important tactical decision of the twentieth century'. Had he taken the starboard line, he would have sailed towards the massed guns of the German High Seas Fleet. Jellicoe's decision reversed the situation. Scheer, believing he was chasing down only Beatty's cruisers, suddenly found himself sailing towards the massed guns of the most powerful navy in the world. His fleet was already taking a dreadful pounding.

Key:

Jellicoe

Scheer

Beatty

Hipper

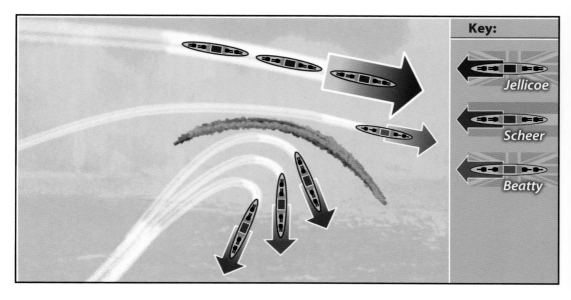

**Key:**

Jellicoe

Scheer

Beatty

**18.30:** facing almost certain annihilation, Scheer carried out a brilliant manoeuvre. He ordered his
26 whole battle fleet to turn about at the same time, make smoke to conceal their whereabouts and sail
at full speed in the opposite direction (south-west) away from Jellicoe's guns.

HMS *Malaya* in Scapa Flow, 10th June 1934. She suffered eight hits at the Battle of Jutland **27** but survived the war and was scrapped at Faslane in 1948.

**19.10:** for a reason never explained, Scheer turned back again and sailed for a second time into the British guns. This time Jellicoe was able to 'cross the German T'. Only the forward guns of the leading German ships were able to fire on the British fleet – the German ships further back were too far away to reach the British ships. Conversely, the British fleet was able to concentrate overwhelming fire on the leading German ships and almost all their guns could fire on the German fleet simultaneously.

**19.17:** this time, turning away alone would not save him, so Scheer also ordered a mass torpedo attack on the British fleet by his remaining destroyers. It was a desperate gamble.

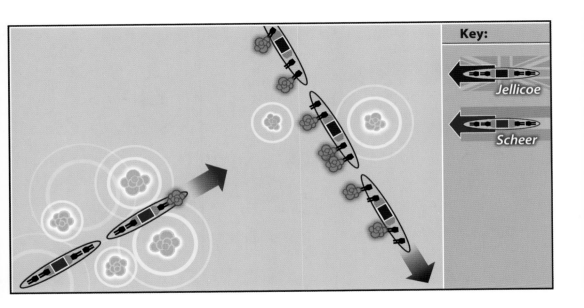

Key:

Jellicoe

Scheer

**19.21**: at this moment, Jellicoe took the decision that would ensure that he could never win the battle. Jellicoe was extremely cautious of torpedoes and his instinct was to turn away, as he mistakenly believed that the Germans had developed torpedoes that left no trail of bubbles as they moved through the water and would therefore be undetectable. So he turned his whole battle fleet away, allowing Scheer to escape from view and beyond the range of his guns. Had Jellicoe instead turned towards Scheer at this point (see following page), he would have inflicted heavy losses on the German fleet – possibly even routed them and, at the very least, butchered the German battle-cruisers. Although heavily criticised for this action, a turn towards the attack, whilst more aggressive, also increased the risk of British losses – a risk Jellicoe did not need to take.

Despite losing contact with the German High Seas Fleet, Jellicoe was well placed between Scheer and the German fleet's harbour at Wilhelmshaven. He therefore headed generally south in order to cut off Scheer's escape route. Unfortunately, night began to fall and Scheer was able to slip past the British Grand Fleet in the darkness and reach the safety of his home ports. Jellicoe had no option but to begin the long journey home.

So who, if anyone, won? The battle petered out in the darkness with neither side having gained a clear advantage. If judged purely on loss of ships and lives, the Germans could claim victory as they lost 11 ships and 2,551 personnel to the British losses of 14 ships with 6,097 personnel killed – about 10% of the total number of British sailors involved. On the other hand, the German High Seas Fleet had suffered more long-term damage and, importantly, Admiral Scheer's plan to exterminate Beatty's battle-cruisers had failed, with just three having been sunk.

**Key:**

Jellicoe

Scheer

In addition to the number of their ships sunk, several surviving German ships were so badly damaged that they took months to repair.

The battle showed up some weaknesses in the British fleet's ships and equipment. The Royal Navy's emphasis on faster vessels with larger guns was at the expense of defensive armour. Thus the British losses of major ships were sudden and spectacular, due to their inability to stand up to German shells which were able to pierce the British ships' magazine holds, resulting in massive explosions. Whereas, the British armour-piercing shells tended to explode outside the German ships' defensive armour instead of actually penetrating and exploding within the body of the ship. As a result, some German ships with relatively light armour were able to survive direct hits.

The Grand Fleet's return to Scapa Flow was a subdued affair, presumably due to their commander's recognition that a claim of victory would be questionable. Men on the Flotta gun battery watched their arrival in the dawn of 2nd June: no bands were playing, no flags were flying – an appearance more of defeat than victory. However, and despite the British losses, Admiral Jellicoe was able to report that twenty-four battleships were ready for action at just four hours' notice on the day following the battle.

German newspapers naturally claimed a glorious victory based on the number of ships sunk. However, the most significant consequence of the battle was that, with one (abortive) exception in August 1916, the German High Seas Fleet did not put to sea again for the rest of World War I and the Royal Navy's British Grand Fleet continued to remain in command of the sea.

**Action Jellicoe could have taken**

**Actual event**

19.21: alternative scenario. **33**

## Lord Kitchener and the sinking of HMS *Hampshire*

Horatio Herbert Kitchener was born at Listovel in County Kerry, Ireland, in June 1850. In 1868 he attended the Royal Military Academy at Woolwich and in 1870 took a commission in the Royal Engineers where he specialized in surveying and intelligence work. In 1890 he became Commander-in-Chief of the Egyptian Army and in 1898, commanding an army of British, Egyptian and Sudanese troops, defeated the Dervishes at the Battle of Omdurman. In 1900 Kitchener took command of the British Army in the South African Boer War and led the British to victory in 1902. He was made Viscount and took the title Lord Kitchener of Khartoum. In 1902, as a Field Marshal, he took command of the Indian Army and later became Consul-General in Egypt. On the outbreak of the First World War Kitchener was made Minister for War in Lloyd George's Government.

In June 1916 Lord Kitchener embarked on a secret mission to the Tsar of Russia. The mission was intended to discuss munitions supplies and boost the morale of the Russians who were under severe pressure from the German Armies of the Eastern Front. He arrived at Scapa Flow on 5th June 1916 with the intention of sailing that day to Archangel in Russia on the cruiser HMS *Hampshire*. As a strong north-east wind was blowing it was decided that *Hampshire* should sail up the west coasts of Orkney and Shetland so as to be in the lee of the gale. This decision was to prove fatal as, on 29th May, the German submarine U-75 had laid 22 mines off the west coast of Orkney with the purpose of blocking one of the exits from Scapa Flow.

HMS *Hampshire*. She was commissioned in 1905 and fought at the Battle of Jutland **35**

At 5.45pm on 5th June, the *Hampshire* slipped her mooring buoy and sailed out of Scapa Flow escorted by two destroyers, *Unity* and *Victor*. The plan was that they should escort *Hampshire* for the first 200 miles but the sea around Hoy was so rough that the destroyers were soon ordered back to Scapa Flow. At approximately 8.45pm *Hampshire* struck a mine near Marwick Head and sank within 15 minutes. After the mine exploded life-rafts were launched, but these were overloaded and many sailors died of exposure in the raging seas or perished when the rafts were smashed against the rocks and cliffs of the treacherous coastline. Of the ship's company, only 12 survived. Recent research has revealed that the final death toll was 737. Kitchener's body was never recovered.

Much has been said and written about the official reaction to the *Hampshire's* sinking, much of it critical, such as vessels not being allowed to sail to the rescue and local Orcadians being prevented from trying to assist from the shore. The great majority of those accounts are now thought – and in some cases known – to be inaccurate. Several vessels were in fact despatched from Stromness, although their ability to provide meaningful assistance in the storm conditions prevailing would have been very limited. It may also have been the case that the authorities simply did not want to risk further loss of life in the terrible weather.

The bodies of the crew that were recovered were taken to Lyness Naval Cemetery for burial. In 1926 the Kitchener Memorial was erected at Marwick Head. It has been enhanced for the commemoration of the centenary of this event in June 2016.

Orkney's shores are frequently battered by storms and this scene is indicative of the conditions
prevailing when HMS *Hampshire* was sunk.

**38** Left: the Kitchener Memorial and Marwick Head silhouetted against the light when viewed from the north. Right: close-up of the 15m/48ft tall Memorial.

Marwick Head and the Kitchener Memorial from the south.

40  Panoramic view looking east from Cuilags on Hoy with the island of Graemsay in the centre of
the picture. Orkney's Mainland is beyond. As for the sea areas, Hoy Sound and Burra Sound are

between Hoy and Graemsay, the Bay of Ireland is at upper left, Clestrain Sound is behind Graemsay
and the Bring Deeps are on the right behind the cairn, with Scapa Flow off to the right.

## The early days of air power

When the First World War began, only 11 years had elapsed since the Wright brothers made the first powered flight and, just five years previously, Louis Bleriot's first flight over the English Channel had been made. Yet aircraft technology had advanced so quickly that the Royal Naval Air Service was established in July 1914. At the start of the First World War the RNAS had three seaplanes and two land-based aircraft ready for action at Scapa Flow. After a period at Nether Scapa, their base was moved to Houton on the southern coast of Orkney's Mainland. Their main role was to spot the German U-boats, but thoughts soon turned to how this new technology might be developed into a more offensive role. Since 1912 seaplanes had been carried on the specially converted HMS *Hermes*, which arrived in Scapa Flow in 1913 with two aircraft aboard. They were launched from the ship with catapult assistance but had to land in the sea by the ship and were then winched back aboard.

Another early seaplane carrier with Orkney connections was HMS *Engadine*. She was converted in 1914 from a former cross-channel steamer and initially carried three seaplanes. In 1915 she was modified to house four such aircraft and then served with the Grand Fleet until 1917. She took part in the Battle of Jutland where one of her seaplanes sighted Admiral Hipper's cruiser, but the *Engadine* failed to pass on the aircraft's wireless reports. Later in the battle, she took the stricken cruiser HMS *Warrior* in tow and saved 600 lives when *Warrior* sank.

HMS *Engadine*, a very early example of an aircraft carrier. **43**

A subsequent development came with HMS *Furious*, built by Armstrong Whitworth and launched on 15th August 1916. Ordered as a light battle-cruiser, she was converted to an aircraft carrier after launching and commissioned on 26th June 1917. She had a complement of five Sopwith Pups and three Short 184 seaplanes. As the Pups were not seaplanes, a landing field was laid out at Smoogro, Orkney. Although not intended for aircraft landings, *Furious* had an aircraft deck and the naval pilots began to wrestle with the question of whether they could land a Pup on this deck as well as take off from it!

They calculated that if the ship was sailing into a headwind of 25 knots at full speed, a deck landing could be accomplished. On 2nd August, Squadron Commander Edwin Dunning took off to put the theory to the test. Although conditions were not quite perfect, Dunning succeeded in approaching the deck, holding the plane at just above stall speed and touching down so that his colleagues could grab the plane and bring it to a halt. Dunning made a second successful attempt on 7th August, but during a third trial later that day, disaster struck. After three attempts to land, from all of which he pulled out at the last minute, on the fourth approach he attempted to touch down, but a sudden gust of wind caught the plane and toppled it to starboard, causing it to fall into the sea. Apparently, Dunning was knocked out by the blow and drowned before he could be rescued. But despite the tragedy, the point had been made that a plane could land on a ship and lessons were learned about how to achieve this safely. HMS *Furious* was rebuilt with a landing deck of appropriate length and the progress of the aircraft carrier concept took a step closer to that with which we are now familiar.

The aircraft carrier HMS *Implacable* in Scapa Flow. A descendant of early attempts of this technology **45** as described opposite, she was built by Fairfields Shipbuilders in Glasgow and launched in 1942.

# The tragedy of HMS *Vanguard*

It's bad enough to lose men and ships to enemy action, but somehow even worse to lose them as the result of an accident. Such was the fate of HMS *Vanguard*. She was anchored in Scapa Flow on the evening of 9th July 1917. Witnesses – for the sight of these ships was always attracting someone's attention – related how she suddenly shuddered, rose in the middle and released an eruption of smoke and fire that formed a lurid mushroom cloud. Then the sound waves from this immense explosion shattered the peace of the Flow. Large amounts of debris, including a whole gun turret, were hurled into the air. Most of this landed in the surrounding waters, but she had been anchored close to the island of Flotta, where hot metal from the ship set fire to vegetation.

For some time the authorities did not know what had happened as no alarm signal had been received. Just which ship was missing had to be established by a process of elimination – when no reply was received from *Vanguard* it was realised that she was the victim. The explosion killed 843 men and one succumbed later, leaving only two survivors. The cause was put down to unstable cordite that exploded spontaneously, as this had been identified as the cause of a few previous incidents, such as that which beset HMS *Natal* in 1915.

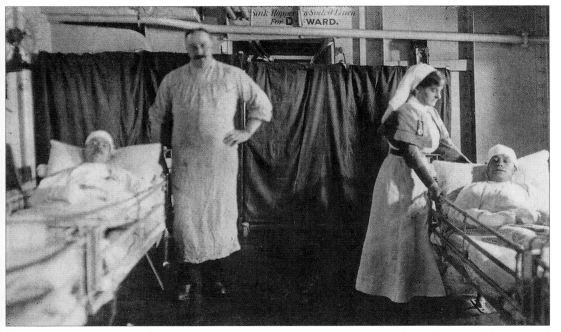

The two survivors of HMS *Vanguard* disaster. **47**

## The German fleet at the end of World War One

When World War One ended in 1918, the terms of the Armistice included the requirement that the German naval vessels should be interned in neutral or allied ports. After due consideration, it was decided that Scapa Flow was the most suitable location for the 74 German surface ships to which the terms of the Armistice applied. These terms forbade the Germans from destroying their ships (it would be easy to scuttle them), so a secure location in an allied territory was essential. Preparations were hastily made and on 21st November the German fleet set sail across the North Sea to Scotland. By 27th November they had all arrived in Scapa Flow.

Even with only skeleton crews aboard, the total number of German sailors required amounted to some 5,000 men, under the command of Rear-Admiral Ludwig von Reuter. They then had to endure months of tedium and deprivation aboard their vessels while the terms of the Versailles Peace Treaty were worked out. Sure enough, these terms included the demand that the interned ships be handed over to the allies. Royal Navy officers were aware that the Germans might scuttle the ships to avoid having to surrender them, but under the conditions of internment they could not take any action to prevent it. And indeed, with the 21st June deadline for acceptance of the peace terms approaching, Rear-Admiral Reuter got word to his senior officers to be ready to scuttle their ships. He confirmed the order on the morning of 21st June. From around midday to late afternoon, all the German ships went down, some sinking completely while others remained partly visible in shallower waters.

German Battle Cruiser "DERFFLINGER"
four minutes before finally sinking, 2.45 p.m., 21-6-1919.
COPYRIGHT, C. W. BURROWS

The German battleship SMS *Derfflinger* slips under the water while being scuttled **49** in Scapa Flow, June 1919.

However, instead of being the end of these vessels, it sparked the beginning of an extraordinary salvage exercise that would continue until the outbreak of World War Two and which was only completed after that conflict. First to go were those that were beached rather than sunk and first of all was a destroyer bought locally by the Stromness Salvage Syndicate in 1922. The following year, Orcadian JW Robertson won a contract from the Admiralty for the salvage of four destroyers.

But it was when English firm Cox & Danks became involved that the salvage operation acquired greater sophistication and reached industrial proportions. Various techniques were used, depending on the ship's size and location. One method was to pass hawsers, attached to a floating dock, under the vessel being salvaged and slowly winch it up. This worked for smaller ships but had its limits. Another technique was to inflate large, heavy-duty balloons inside the sunken vessel so as to restore its buoyancy by inflating the balloons. It was necessary to prepare each ship by sending down divers to close sea-cocks and patch any holes. When it came to the largest ships, once holes were patched, water would be pumped out or compressed air pumped in. The latter required a further level of engineering in the form of air-locks which had to be attached to the ship being raised. The biggest of all, the battle-cruiser *Hindenburg*, was raised in 1926 but promptly sank again due to an ill-timed gale. She remained on the sea-bed until a much later successful attempt re-floated her in 1930. During the 1920s and 1930s a total of 38 ships were salvaged, yielding 327,000 tons of steel.

SMS *Hindenburg* pictured after being re-floated in Scapa Flow. **51**

Seydlitz nach der Skagerrack-Schlacht.

**52** SMS *Seydlitz* came close to sinking at the Battle of Jutland and is low in the water in this picture. She finally went under the waves in Scapa Flow along with the rest of the German fleet.

## The establishment of Lyness Naval Base

A consequence of basing the Grand Fleet in Scapa Flow was the need to install the necessary logistical support and infrastructure. By early 1916 it was apparent that a floating base was no longer adequate to meet its needs. In 1917, a wharf was constructed at Lyness where stores could be unloaded. In addition, four 8,000–ton fuel oil storage tanks, petrol tanks, a power house and depots for torpedoes and paravanes were constructed, along with storage sheds and workers' camps. Oil firing of ships was still quite new in the First World War, most of them being coal fired.

In 1937, construction work started on twelve 12,000–ton capacity surface oil storage tanks to supplement those built in 1917. Although surface storage tanks were relatively quick to construct they were vulnerable to air attack. It was therefore decided to construct underground fuel tanks beneath the hill called Wee Fea and work started in 1938. Six tanks were built, capable of holding a total of 101,000 tons of fuel. Two pump houses were also constructed. By 1940 there were over 12,000 military and civilian personnel at Lyness. In effect, this made it the largest 'town' in Orkney – even today, Kirkwall's population is only about 9,300. At the beginning of World War Two, medical services and recreational facilities were very poor, but were improved substantially in 1941. A cinema and theatre were built and shows featuring famous stars were organised. The Royal Navy pulled out of Lyness in early 1945, leaving a skeleton staff to run the base, which closed in 1957.

The Scapa Flow Visitor Centre is housed in one of the former oil-pumping stations of the Lyness Naval Base and is one of Orkney's premier visitor destinations. Allow several hours to make the most of your visit.

**54** One of the 'Lancashire' type boilers in the pump house at Scapa Flow Visitor Centre, Lyness. They were converted to oil firing, but the original stoking flues can still be seen in the doors.

Triple-expansion duplex steam-powered Worthington oil pumps pumped the heavy fuel oil **55** from the tankers up into the storage tanks or down into the ships.

**56** Much of Orkney is naturally defended by the impregnability of its coastline. Nowhere is this better demonstrated than on the west coast of Hoy, where the Old Man of Hoy stands guard at 137m/449ft.

**58** The north tunnel and oil pipe at Lyness which led to the underground storage tanks.

A gun retrieved from HMS *Hampshire* on display at Scapa Flow Visitor Centre. **59**

**60** A dramatic display of light and eerie shadows in the preserved tank at Scapa Flow Visitor Centre. Centre-stage is a Bofors 40mm anti-aircraft gun capable of firing 80 rounds a minute.

Outdoor exhibits at Scapa Flow Visitor Centre. In the foreground is a rail-mounted crane. **61**
Lyness had its own railway network during World War Two.

## The sinking of the *Royal Oak*

The 30,000–ton battleship HMS *Royal Oak* had a long association with Orkney. Launched in November 1914 and commissioned in May 1916, she was brand new when she saw her first action at the Battle of Jutland. By the Second World War she was therefore no longer a modern fighting ship, but remained a significant part of the Royal Navy.

Although Scapa Flow was an excellent natural harbour, the number of channels linking it to the open sea meant it was vulnerable to attack by enemy vessels. To deal with this threat, floating booms were laid across the channels that were opened and closed by tug boats as and when required. They were supplemented by the use of block ships, obsolete vessels that were sunk in the channels to create obstacles intended to keep enemy submarines out. But these measures fell short of providing comprehensive protection, especially with 11 possible routes into the heart of Scapa Flow.

In the early days of the Second World War, German commanders were looking for the opportunity of a strike against Britain that would give them a propaganda advantage and inflict a psychological blow against British morale. Admiral Karl Dönitz, head of the Kriegsmarine's U-boats, believed a successful attack on Scapa Flow would meet this objective. Dönitz personally selected U-boat captain Günther Prien of U-47 for the mission.

HMS *Royal Oak* carries out test firing of its guns off Orkney. **63**

On arriving in Orkney waters and slipping into Scapa Flow on the night of the 13th–14th October 1939, Prien found fewer ships than expected, but *Royal Oak* was at anchor and provided the ideal target. Of the first four torpedoes fired, only one found its mark and caused so little damage that *Royal Oak*'s crew did not appear to realise that they were under attack. At 1.16am a further three torpedoes were fired which hit *Royal Oak* amidships, causing huge damage. The explosion ripped through her and caused a severe list to starboard. At 1.29, just 13 minutes after being hit, *Royal Oak* capsized and sank. Out of a crew of 1,234, 834 men and boys were killed, leaving only 401 survivors. Of these, 386 were rescued by the tender Daisy 2 that had been moored alongside *Royal Oak* but was cast free as the ship begun to list. The others managed to swim to shore, at least half-a-mile away. *Royal Oak* had a high proportion of boy sailors aged 14–18 among her crew, 163 in all, of whom 126 (77%) were lost. After this it was generally recognised that under–18s should not serve on warships.

Today the *Royal Oak* is a recognised war grave. Every year on 14th October a team of specialist Royal Navy divers descends to the wreck and flies the Royal Ensign above the overturned hull in memory of those lost in the attack.

The crew of HMS *Royal Oak*, so many of whom would be lost. **65**

**66** Members of *Royal Oak's* crew busy painting the ship. Present-day Health & Safety officials would probably not approve!

HMS *Royal Oak*'s bell was salvaged from the wreck and is preserved as part of a memorial to the ship and its crew in St Magnus Cathedral in Kirkwall.

**68** St Magnus Cathedral has stood in Kirkwall for more than 800 years. Building began in 1137 under Rognvald, nephew of St Magnus.

A westerly view from St Margaret's Hope towards Scapa Flow. St Margaret's Hope (bay) is where **69** King Håkon's fleet paused on its way to the Battle of Largs in 1263.

## The Churchill Barriers

Within a month of the sinking of *Royal Oak*, Winston Churchill visited Orkney and ordered that work begin on the construction of four permanent barriers that would link Mainland in the north with Lamb Holm, Glimps Holm, Burray and South Ronaldsay. With these in place, Scapa Flow would have solid defences down its eastern side. Work began in May 1940 but due to the scale of the task was not completed until May 1945, ironically as the war came to an end. The Churchill Barriers were formally opened on 12th May by the First Lord of the Admiralty.

Much of the work was done by the 1,300 or so Italian prisoners of war who were housed on Burray and Lamb Holm. The other lasting monument they left behind is the Italian Chapel, a masterpiece of creative ingenuity in the way such fine art was crafted from such mundane materials. The chapel served the camp on Lamb Holm and remains a huge draw for today's visitors to Orkney.

The barriers were constructed by the use of gabions, wire cages filled with locally quarried rocks which were dropped into the channel. Approximately 40,000 cubic metres of rock were deposited in the water, which was up to 70ft deep, using a system of overhead cableways. The rocks were overlaid with 300,000 tons of concrete blocks, cast locally in Orkney. These materials were brought to the sites by specially built narrow-gauge railways. Today, the three northerly barriers still look much as they did when built, although the roads that cross them have been upgraded. The fourth, most southerly, barrier (No. 4) no longer looks artificial as sand dunes have built up on its eastern side, in effect linking the islands of Burray and South Ronaldsay. The combined length of the four barriers amounts to almost 1.75 miles.

This aerial view shows Churchill Barriers 1–3, connecting, from bottom of picture, **71**
Mainland to Lamb Holm, Lamb Holm to Glimps Holm and Glimps Holm to Burray.

**72** Barrier No. 3, showing the rather chaotic, but obviously sturdy, nature of the concrete block construction method. Some of the block ships remain in the channels by the barriers and have

become a major attraction, bringing divers and tourists from far and wide.

**74** The formation of sand dunes on the east side of Barrier No. 4 is most clearly seen from the air.

Close-up of one of the block ships, with the high-tide line clearly visible. **75**
Vegetation has established itself further up.

# The Italian Chapel

This lovely chapel is known as the Italian Chapel because it was built by Italian prisoners of war during World War Two. Camp 60 on Lamb Holm housed 500 men, who had been sent to Orkney to help build the Churchill Barriers. They had very little to work with when creating the Chapel, other than two old Nissen huts, unwanted scrap and some concrete. What they created is quite astounding – a unique and wonderful place which is an inspiration to all who visit.

At first, the camp consisted of thirteen or so cheerless huts, but the active Italians made concrete paths and planted flowers, until the whole area was transformed. To preside over the camp 'square' an artistic prisoner, Domenico Chiocchetti, made the figure of St George, built up from a framework of barbed wire covered with cement. New amenities were created, such as a theatre and a recreation hut, but one thing the camp still lacked – a chapel. This lack had been deeply felt by the prisoners, and the provision of one had been urged by the War Office Inspector of P.O.W. Camps. Some months passed, until a fortunate combination of circumstances brought together a new commandant, Major TP Buckland, an enthusiastic padre, Father P Gioacchino Giacobazzi and Domenico Chiocchetti.

Late in 1943 two Nissen huts were made available to the prisoners. These were placed end to end and joined together. The original plan was to use one hut as a school and the other as a church. With the commandant's blessing, Chiocchetti set to work to build a sanctuary in the end of the hut furthest from the camp. His ideas had to be expressed in terms of the simplest material, most of it second-hand and a proportion of it apparently worthless scrap. The unsightly corrugated iron of the hut was hidden by plasterboard, smooth above, panelled below.

The altar, altar-rail and holy water stoop, all beautifully designed, were moulded in concrete. Behind the altar and reaching up to the sanctuary roof, Chiocchetti's masterpiece, the Madonna and Child, were lovingly depicted, based on a holy picture he had carried with him all through the war.

The contrast between the completed chancel and the rest of the hut was so great that a rood-screen was made to segregate the sacred from the mundane. Having created such a lovely sanctuary, the rest of the hut seemed uninviting by comparison, so it was decided to beautify the whole interior. The commandant secured enough plasterboard to line the building completely. This was fixed to a wooden framework, leaving an air space between the iron of the hut and the plasterboard. Chiocchetti's idea was to paint the whole interior to resemble brickwork, with a dado along the base of the curved walls, which would imitate carved stone.

Figure of St George outside the Italian Chapel built from barbed wire and concrete.  77

**78** The Sanctuary at the Italian Chapel. The paintings in the windows flanking the Madonna and Child mural represent St Catherine of Siena and St Francis of Assisi.

This elaborate conception was too great for one man to execute, so a painter was sent from another camp to work under Chiocchetti's direction. As the chancel had made the interior look mean, so by contrast did the interior make the outside of the chapel seem unsightly. So the next step was to create an impressive façade to hide the utilitarian outline of the huts. Immaculately maintained, this is the face of the chapel we still see today.

The façade of the Italian Chapel disguises the utilitarian form of the Nissen hut behind.

## Hoxa Head defences

The southern approaches to Scapa Flow are the most vulnerable, the widest channel being the Sound of Hoxa between the islands of South Ronaldsay and Flotta. This is approximately 1.5 miles across at its narrowest point, between Hoxa Head on South Ronaldsay and Stranger Head on Flotta. In both World Wars submarines and fast attack boats posed a real threat to ships at anchor in the Flow. Therefore short-range, rapid-fire guns were installed at Hoxa Head and on the east coast of Flotta. Balfour Battery was built on Hoxa Head and Buchanan Battery on Flotta. A boom was stretched across the sea between these batteries.

German submarines trying to enter the Flow through Hoxa Sound faced an anti-submarine net barrier as well as patrols from aircraft and small surface warships. Electric induction loops could detect the metal hulls of surface or submerged vessels and were supported by controlled minefields which could be remotely detonated to destroy them. Surfaced submarines or torpedo boats trying to sneak in at night would have been caught on the spiked booms that supported the submarine nets. Radar-directed searchlights and guns would then have destroyed them in seconds. In the end, however, none of the guns fired a shot in anger; the defences were so strong that they formed a complete deterrent.

Balfour Battery's first guns were an emergency stop-gap – a pair of 12–pounder guns dating from 1894 was placed there in March 1940. Most of what remains to be seen today, however, is the later and much more lethal 'twin-six' battery which was built in the winter of 1940–41. The twin 6–pounder (57mm) was the most advanced coastal artillery gun of its day, capable of firing 72 rounds a minute in the hands of a skilled crew.

The gun emplacements at Balfour Battery, Hoxa Head. The remains of ancillary buildings **81** can also be seen on the hillside.

The twin 6–pounder was very smoky in action so fire was directed from a multi-storey command post which had two observation levels. The guns were directed from the top storey, while the searchlights were controlled from the first floor. To defend the Fleet against night attacks, the guns were supported by radar and searchlights mounted in emplacements on the cliff top. Further ancillary buildings included the gun crew shelters and engine rooms where the diesel generators provided power for the searchlights and the guns. Balfour Battery remained operational until July 1945 when it was mothballed. The guns were removed in 1950.

When visiting Balfour Battery, don't stop there if you have time to explore all the defences on Hoxa Head. Continue south along the cliff-top, passing a series of geos – linear clefts in the cliff, which are common in gently dipping flagstones and sandstones that often result in spectacular landforms. Zig-zagging in and out of these features, the obvious path eventually rounds Hoxa Head, topped with the sprawling Hoxa Battery. Whereas Balfour Battery was designed to defend the Sound of Hoxa, this battery had a wider remit stretching out into the Pentland Firth.

Hoxa Battery was built on the southern-most tip of Hoxa Head from where shipping in the Pentland Firth could be monitored.

**84** Left: close-up of a gun pit at Balfour Battery, Hoxa Head. The guns were mounted on a turntable arrangement. Right: the entrance to an underground store at Balfour Battery.

Looking across the Sound of Hoxa to the extensive remains of Buchanan Battery **85** on the Isle of Flotta.

## Ness Battery

Having looked at Scapa Flow's southern defences, we now turn our attention to the protection of its north-westerly approaches.

Ness Battery, just west of Stromness, played a vital part in the defence of the western approaches to Scapa Flow in both world wars. Today it remains one of the best-preserved wartime sites in Britain and is the only coast battery to have retained the wooden huts of its accommodation camp. One of these, the Mess Hall, contains a remarkable example of wartime art – a painted mural depicting rural England.

At the outbreak of World War One, virtually nothing had been done about defending Scapa Flow from enemy vessels. However, four 12–pounder guns were soon landed to protect Hoy Sound while a guard ship carrying 6-inch guns was anchored off the island of Graemsay. In 1915 these defences were supplemented by the arrival of seven new American-made 5- and 6-inch guns. These were shared between three new batteries built on the Stromness side of Hoy Sound, which were named Hoy Nos. 1–3. Some remains of Hoy No. 2 Battery can still be seen among the World War Two structures of Ness Battery.

The deterrent effect of Orkney's anti-ship defences appears to have been effective, as the German Navy did not mount an attack on Scapa Flow with surface vessels during WW1. Consequently these guns were not fired in anger, but were regularly used for practice. After the war they were dismantled and removed or scrapped. This de-armament proved premature as, with Adolf Hitler in power in Germany from 1933, the threat of war was once again real by 1938. In Orkney, two new Territorial units were raised to man the coast batteries. In 1939, once it was confirmed that

Accommodation huts at Ness Battery, Stromness. **87**

**88** This wide-angle view gives an idea of the layout of the main features at Ness Battery; No. 1 Gun Emplacement can be seen on the left and No. 2 Emplacement prominent on the right.

For the view from one of these emplacements see p.92. Between the emplacements stands the Battery Observation Post – see also p.91.

Scapa Flow would be the main base of the Home Fleet, the pace of work was stepped up, including the establishment of Ness Battery on the site of the previous Hoy No. 2 Battery. However, this was not complete by the time war was declared on 3rd September 1939, although the battery had guns ready to fire by this date. Completion came in the spring of 1940. The guns were housed in concrete emplacements and ammunition stored in underground magazines.

Around this time, air raids intensified, with German bombers targeting Royal Navy ships. But by now, anti-aircraft cover, known as the Scapa Barrage, was very effective and, faced with heavy losses of aircraft, the Luftwaffe's attacks became few and far between.

The Battery Observation Post was the nerve centre of operations, co-ordinating the seaward defences of Hoy Sound. It housed the rangefinder, which could be quickly used to calculate the range of a target by measuring the downward angle from its known, fixed height. This information was passed to the gun emplacements via cables to dials below the guns. The Searchlight Directing Station was also located in the Observation Post and was able to operate the searchlights down by the shore by remote control. The Fire Command was another key element of the Observation Post. From here the fire of all six batteries of 534 Coast Regiment could be co-ordinated. Later in the war, Ness Battery was equipped with radar, mounted on the roof of the Fire Command.

As in World War 1, the Orkney coast batteries did not have to fire in anger as there were no attacks by surface vessels. Again, the deterrent proved effective. After being closed for many years, Ness Battery is now open for guided tours, led by trained and qualified Orkney tourist guides. See the back of this book for more details.

Battery Observation Post at Ness Battery. Upper floor left: Searchlight Directing Station. **91**
Lower floor left: Observation Post. Upper floor right: Port War Signal Station. Lower right: Fire Command.

**92** The guns of Ness Battery controlled the western entry to Scapa Flow. The huge guns were mounted in pits like this one and could be rotated to allow a wide field of fire.

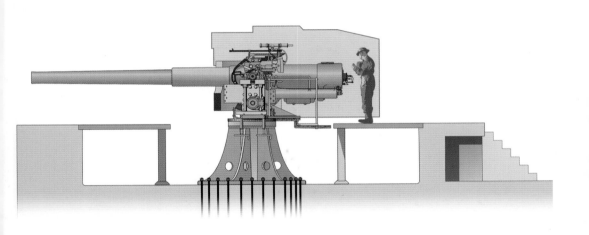

Diagram of a MK VII breech-loading gun as used at Ness Battery that was mounted **93** in one of the gun pits like the example shown opposite.

**94** A restored section of the mural painted around the walls of the Mess Hall at Ness Battery.

## Legacy of love

As this book is about war and the many horrors it inflicts, it seems fitting, especially at a time of commemoration, to end with words that speak of love and reconciliation. In 1960, Domenico Chiocchetti, creator of the Italian Chapel, returned to Orkney to restore his work. Before he left, he wrote this letter to the people of Orkney:

Dear Orcadians – My work at the chapel is finished. In these three weeks I have done my best to give again to the little church that freshness which it had sixteen years ago. The chapel is yours – for you to love and preserve. I take with me to Italy the remembrance of your kindness and wonderful hospitality. I shall remember always, and my children shall learn from me to love you. I thank the authorities of Kirkwall, the courteous preservation committee, and all those who directly or indirectly have collaborated for the success of this work and for having given me the joy of seeing again the little chapel of Lamb Holm where I, in leaving, leave a part of my heart. Thanks also in the name of all my companions of Camp 60 who worked with me. Goodbye dear friends of Orkney – or perhaps I should say just "au revoir".

Published 2017 by Lyrical Scotland, an imprint of Lomond Books Ltd, Broxburn, EH52 5NF. Reprinted 2019.
www.lyricalscotland.com  www.lomondbooks.com

Originated by Ness Publishing, 47 Academy Street, Elgin, Moray, IV30 1LR
(First published 2016 by Ness Publishing)

Printed in China

Picture credits: pp.1, 7, 8/9, 15, 23, 27, 35, 45, 47, 49, 51, 63, 65, 66 © Orkney Library & Archive;
pp.11, 19, 20, 43 & 52 © Imperial War Museum; pp.17, 18, 21, 22, 25, 26, 29, 31 & 33 © Mark Davies
www.battle-of-jutland.com; p.67 © St Magnus Cathedral; pp. 71 & 74 © The Orcadian Photo Archive;
pp.87 & 88-89 © Andrew Hollinrake; p.93 © Iain Ashman; all other photographs © Colin and Eithne Nutt.

Text © Colin Nutt, except where indicated – see over
ISBN 978-1-78818-010-8

Front cover: HMS *Hampshire* in Hoy Sound (composite image); p.1: King George V inspecting a naval vessel;
p.4: Kitchener poster; this page: WW2 look-out post on Hoxa Head; back cover: Balfour Battery, Hoxa Head.